the flap pamphlet series

Mercy

open, read, turn

Mercy

the flap pamphlet series (No. 24)
Printed and Bound in the United Kingdom

Published by the flap series, 2021
the pamphlet series of flipped eye publishing
All Rights Reserved

Cover Design by Petraski
Series Design © flipped eye publishing, 2010

Author Photo courtesy of author
First Edition
Copyright © Eleanor Penny 2021

A version of 'Mercy' was published in *Ambit Magazine*, Issue 241.

A version of 'ant poison' was published in *Bath Magg*, Issue 5.

'Winter, a Biography' won the Poetry London Prize 2020, and was first published in *Poetry London Magazine*, Autumn 2020.

'The Dogs' won the Verve Poetry Prize 2020, and was first published in the *Verve Poetry Festival Anthology 2020*.

ISBN-13: 978-1-905233-69-4

For Jane, who talks to the birds.

Mercy

Eleanor Penny

"We linger on the field's green edge
and say, *Someday son, none of this
will be yours.* Miracles are all around"
- *Ada Limon*

" 'One, two.. Mercury in the Second House... the moon has set... six-misfortune...
evening-seven...' Then he announced loudly and joyously, 'Your head will be cut
off!' "
- *Mikhail Bulgakov*

"I'm tired of everybody touching me"
- *Britney Spears*

Contents | *Mercy*

The dogs
After Helen Mort

Before you were born your mother too was visited by dogs. They asked her how she kept the hair from her eyes when she committed small atrocities. What blood type was her blood type. How her neck smelled in the rain. They told her it's not wrong to want a child who fights for its food. Sinks its teeth into the ankle of the world. Sleeps in the sun, vendetta-less, untroubled by strange men. Spit from its jaws pooling on the stone for anyone to see. It's alright to want a child who will recognise its name. Who will come home when you call it. She ate coal in the back garden, squatting by the bucket, furnace-handed. Brittle-tongued. She couldn't spell the word belief, but every day she practised. Ate without her hands. Cut her palms on street glass. Healed quickly. Patched up each violation. She learned to want some kind of child who would answer to its name. At least you know now. Show her you can sink your teeth into something and hold on. Fill her house with howling. Dig up flower bulbs and chicken bones and bring them to her door. It was morning at last when she ran with the dogs. She ran to the gutters and gave birth there in the gasping light, bloodwaters sluicing off into the drain. Still across the city she is calling. At least now you know.

Ant poison

the girl in the elevator smells like him   but I say nothing
I cannot have her catch me   noticing the tumult
of her body   we have nearly exhausted   the ant poison
they drag it all to their homes   we do not need
to persuade the ants   of anything   not any more   I always look
like she does   ghosted in the windows of the night kitchen
my bare arms shake   like hers do   boiled in her shell
with unspent sleep   across her open eyes   a troop of ants
feet jellied   sclera   cornea   vitreous humour   things grow
well here   in the smear of light   like germs   like seeing
the same movie over   and over   an ant   has eight eyes
crowning his forehead   eyes   that crawl across the ceiling
of the old house   eyes that crawl into her mouth
when she is sleeping   a blind king   is left   in the corner
ants crowning his forehead   they told him they love him
the king   I mean   she told him she loved him   not the king
I mean   the blue boy   she told him his name   was blue
he had long eyelashes   and his face was painted
like a dog's face   an experiment in recklessness
in shoving fistfuls of dirt   against his gums
a mermaid pulled a sailor   from the chokehold of the sea
she left her nipple in his mouth   I left a pair of naked eggs
on the countertop to cool   in the morning   they were awake
with ants   I know an egg is a dream   I know the whole sky
is covered in ants   I know every star   has six legs
and brings poison home   to its family   how can you live
in a place like this   the world I mean   I see one
dancing on the lip of the butter knife   an ant
the world   it wasn't good enough   she said she saved him
from drowning   in the yolk of a dream   he spent a whole year
scratching at her thighs   as if he might find fish scales there

When angels came

The railway stations in my town were closed down
years ago, to make way for the offices of angels.

Angels remove their boots to wash their ankles in the dark.
They wade into the water. We do not recognise their singing.

They offer no rewards.
They want only what's best for us.

These days there are angels watching over us.
They have listed our dirt in their books of dirt.

I have lost the taste for red meat, says an angel
who knocks three times at my front door.

Some angels draw circles in white anticlockwise on your shoulder blades
so God with his hunting knife will find you even in the dark.

Some angels are bent double on the riverbank, gathering beautiful stones.
I should like to stay here a while, says an angel.

Some angels, giving up their glories, have their wings and want
to close their hands around your neck.

In a dull back room, an angel in a white shirt shows me
a photo of a girl holding a kitten by the throat.

It looks like you, he says, a girl
who strangles cats without reward.

Today, I know I have done wrong. In the photograph her mouth
is twisted like a string of beads on which she counts her prayers.

Some angels have carpet burns on their knees.
Some angels shield their eyes from the sun. It makes no difference.

I sang a song they recognised. I offered them a bowl of milk.
Some angels are just like us and it makes no difference.

I want to stay a while with them, the good unhungry men
with limbs that ache and scarlet in the bitter heights.

Old women with stern words for the angels and bellies
full of meat, they went with all the dirt on their feet

into the city naked, showing nobody their teeth, but
when angels came to them, it made no difference.

For Jonah

Teenagers in the countryside bought flowers for each other and when they killed they killed for fun. Soldiers are in the street now, so I run to join their proclamations. They are attending to the natural order of things. Boys who burn their fingers with intent. Land, the squealing pit of new straw. Animals soundless under a new sky. I'm ready to believe in something. When whales, with their empty car-sized hearts, creep onto the tender shore, mouths helpless and unhinged, I don't know what else they expect of us. We are ready to believe. We drag a clean axe down to the sea. We are attending to the order of things. Last week I bought a piece of whale vertebrae. Seams whittled, dry nerves teased out from the muscle. Every shining part revealed for me. I took it to my house, where I buy flowers for no one. I do my part. Swing a clean axe at the day's neck. Hold its wild head in my lap. I push steel pins into the roots of trees and take my measurements. I do not flinch at the sound of the sea. I sleep under a stiff moon in a tooth-white summer. I note down the names of the men who were swallowed alive. I talk to the spine bone because it's free of meat. I place it at the foot of the bed when I have not done my part. It puckers the sheets into the shape of a mouth about to speak. This is my system of accounting. I don't have to be lonely. These days I'm free of meat and the trees have grown right through the bathroom walls to watch me bending over in the shower. Tell them I'm lucky. Tell them I'm ready to believe in something. If I did not do my part I would be swallowed by the big fish. I would have just these conversations, flat on my back with my toes against an impossible bone. About how I heard the clamour of the marching men and once, I did not run to answer it. How for a short time I failed to buy flowers for no one, or how I killed to kill for purely practical concerns. I will always envy Jonah. I want to lie like that. Always breathing in the water. Always blessed in the belly of the whale.

When we moved to the island

After Claude Cahun

When we moved to the island I expected quietness. But
instead, horses screaming. Horses who with their strong backs
and thistle-ready feet can break most any animal they want to but
who do not want to, standing in a purple field, who watch
wirestripped branches twisted for winter, who watch
the frost, and scream for joy. I lie dreaming in the medicine cabinet,
with the pensive little bottles, aspirin and almond oil.
Roses echo in the hallway, I fall down the stairs into a pit
of more roses. She stands in the harbour water loading the boats
heavy with wheat. I'd been waiting so long. Pinch lips. Cotton
pulled flat over my chest. Training. Head fine-powdered,
crooked back in the sharpest grass. When we met I think we broke
every clean plate in the house and ate off the floor. I couldn't wait
much longer. It was joy. For the ghastliness of love. For the small hours.
All those untender afternoons like the many small soft-salted
bones of the foot, held in the mouth. Now it's night and pure
 and pleasing, and wants to be remembered for drinking
pints of water in a single draft like a dying man. I am become
of love with her. I lay my cheek to the mirror so I can watch her
watching me. I am still learning. Please be patient. I took a photo
of some shoes, empty on a staircase. Hollyhocks lie where
the bare ankles should be. And her face smooth as wax-melt
in the breath of my bulb. Here I am, I am here, I am here.

Vivisection

On a bed of newspaper, a boy genuflects
before the cut-up body of a crow.
Stinking knuckle of a heart, bulb and filament
ballasted brightly to the spine.

Finally he knows why birds are so intelligent.
He too is in love with disaster.
He too is asking the sky
for a thin plate of meat.

> They say
> Core: *an apple, nuclear*
> Cower: *corner*
> Car: *a beckoning, tower of smoke*

They know a lot of many-legged things. They summon dead
insects from the bottom of the water.

They need no revelations. A whole dry summer
watching them fall again again into a field of no grain,
soot mote, devious bone, burst without verdict
from a sky slack and vacant as a sleeping mouth,
wet, brew-bellied, the colour of the memory of beer.

The boy laughs like an empty stomach.
Wipes the scalpel on his collar.
Drags his mattress to the yew tree. Dreams
with a pickled crow-brain in a clean jar in his fist.

In the morning he tugs worms from the earth
with his teeth.

O grandmother we will miss you

We have rung both bells. Voices keen from the sky like water
from a cloth wrung out over the head of a man rehearsing his prayers.
There is dirt on my best yellow dress from kneeling in the street.
Candles shriek and flicker like starving cats slipping off into the dusk.
Each particular leaf has flung its whole body down onto the pile.
The devil white-knuckled on his donkey stumbles by unnoticed.
Snow has come again. Marshy stars drift across an oil slick sky.
Your grandson looks beautiful scaling the tower with a new flag.
He loves it, the great height, the possibility of falling. O grandmother,
if I pull up beside you years ago in a burning car will you climb in
and come with me? Will you roll the windows down onto a still night?
Will you put your fist through the mirror in the hallway?

In my best dreams no one
not even you is hungry.
Every cat in the city has a fish
in its mouth for you.

Mercy

Once when I drew a pig, a pig was brought to my table
gasping on the cusp of an apple. Mercury in retrograde. I liked it.
Aeroplanes stuck through with steeple twisted against the sky
like beetles pinned through the stomach to a blue collecting card.
Churches shivered pinkly on the moor top. Cat's eye. Raw gum.

Look at all the mercy that I had to give. Thin wrists.
Bright over the lake ice beneath a collared moon.
I swear I'd live in the house of the Lord forever.

Can't I still be lovely. Have someone pick the lice from my hair.
Hunger like they hunger for the warmth. Linger like a pig laughs
on the dinner table choking on the green fist of an apple.
Pray like driving rabbits bent-neck from the dirt. Say *I like it*.

Pale wheat-coloured women separated from their shoes pad the shallow grass
indifferent. Feverish. Come raw like summer stalks a field's edge. Just look.

They talk bonny. Cry for milk. Fear nothing. Deserve it. Fling their money
down into the well. Damp their eyeballs with rags. Slack bodied under a heavy sun.
The pig they drove up from a nub died laughing. They welcome the study
of their liver blots. Show us the hairs on their fingers. Heap their trawling nets
and whistles by the door. Talk about home going the way oars talk
to the jealous water. I recognise the water in their voices.
Mercy I warn them, *mercy*.

For days after they came, across the blue hill
little fires sprang up in the night.

The priest

He eats songbirds in the morning so everybody else can sleep. There are so many songbirds in his body. Men dance once for him and then are dead like dogs, all of them, for no reason. Down by the docks he climbed into a boat and headed out for heaven like a thief. No one speaks to the sea anymore. Not the old men, solemn in their skiffs. Not stiff puppet-hearted ships. Not the islands, white as knuckles knocking like a bailiff at a stern grey door. When he punishes, he does it well. Battering both fists at the chest of God. Clutching at his collar. Dawn comes plucked and lovely as a rib. Sometimes he claims that he is dead for hours then dances for no reason like a dog. We know what we've done. Everybody dies from a death sentence for stealing small and useless things. He likes clockwork pieces, broken pencils, lemon peel, costume jewellery, fragments of crockery and glass. Sin like any stain can't be rubbed out. Charcoal on a shoulder blade. Red wine on a book. We see his many birthmarks when he washes in the river. We hear the loud birds in his body. He says pick a knife. Pick a quiet spot. Peel an apple in a single strip. Cut out the living songbirds. The clatter of their wingbeats chase his wet heart down an empty, lightless street.

Lorca to Dali

I
I've heard that sometime soon the officers will come for me and that will be an
 end of it.
The fat blue dreaming knot of us.

He says now he's afraid of touching and afraid of being touched. He woke me
in the night to talk about the fleets of priest-limbed ants that troop the earth
fantastic, blunt-headed mushrooms biting deep, choirs of burnt-bronze beetles
clattering, about the primroses that burst up from the earth beneath him without
warning.

He watches the clock like the outline of a gun in the inside jacket pocket of a man
 he used to know.

He forgets to lock the front door. The doctor says it is not an unusual condition.

II
Maybe when they fling me in the pit with all the others, sometime later with the
finite matters of the dirt repurposed flowers sprung there silent can remind him
of the men he used to know.

Some men smell wonderful in the morning. Some men share their little water.
Some withstand the heat. Some are offerings. Some men wait by the window, and
when guests come round they say look, some men are beautiful. Some carried
with you. Some drowsy and crumpled at the roadside. Some a slow spine of pink.
Some forcing their way through the gate with the rain. Some cut and delivered to
the doorstep in crepe paper. Some turning their faces towards the north.

Poppy heads

I

Sometimes we are bored of grieving. Go swollen through the trees. Hungry into the green. Seek the hollow. Leaf squeal, whipworm shiver. We listen. Termites drive their castles higher to meet the rain. We listen. We do what feels good. Spiders slip backwards out of heaven on a string. We remember it. I pick the heads from the last poppies. Eat them all. Sleep blank as a sheep skull on the blind edge of a hill. Grinning, waiting. I begin to dream again. Hard and blunt as a seed. Somewhere beneath the earth, reaching for water.

II

The midwife's hands are full of honey, bleach, salt. The evening sky cunt-coloured. Day drooping like a lone white glove. Limp hands float on the swell of a stomach. The clarity of wax buoyed up in a bowl of ink. A hungry grinning thing pulled shivering into the world. A smell of iron, soil, stem, the last good water.

Terratoma

The doctor takes a small lump from our mother's uterus. Inside, a perfect jawbone, four molars and a patch of hair. Imagine the gold struts of a swallowed crown. A wax fist of rotten grain. A single lidless eye. Black honeycomb. A shadow at the top of the staircase. Suddenly, a severed head. In the chalk pits we chase each other screaming. Salt in a high wind, it makes the same sound. We warm our fingers in each others' mouths. A bald and jawless boy drifts by our house on the starless western edge of town. He cannot chew his food. He walks into the forest and drinks from the roots. He lies down among the animals. Later, we scratch o's and x's into the stone face of a bored saint who lay down long ago among the animals. We trace our weak hands on the west walls in red paint. We jab forks in the gaps in our fingers, stretched out on the kitchen table. We want him to come back to us. To see the markings we have made for him, and step soundlessly into the game.

Love song with pig heart

At last with a pig's heart I will love better than before. I'll speak when I know what I'm hungry for. I'll hold any rot. I'll scream because I can. Naked without indecence. Strange women will feed me with the flat of their hands and you won't mind it. It will be better that way. Lumbering towards you, you'll think about how pink I am. How gleaming in the silt. How slipping in the silver grime. When I speak I will sound like I'm screaming. And women will still feed me with their hands. I'll notice the taste of liver, salt, soap. Please tell me if the tests are accurate. I'll be here when you look for me. I will be too big to run. I will push my head into your hands when you reach for me over the gate. I will open my jaws and trample the earth soft. I'll go readily. I'll go now and clean myself. You'll see. I'll be perfect from the first. Take a scalpel. Take willow bark. Take lemon, honey. Hold the blade over the fire. Silver, purple, black. Take objects of cabaret. Unwind the gut. Unveil the stomach. The cacophony muscle. Hefted with both hands. Afterwards, eat your meat from the same knife. After an operation, a doctor goes home and lays their hands on their loved ones which means *you will be spared*. I'll know nothing about the future. I'll lie in the mud of a cold field with the moon thick on my rising skin. What could be better? Simple from the first cut. Big swaggering and obvious. Leathered red. Heavy as a bag of teeth. Heavy as a sleepwalker. Soon the smell of winter every year will come as a surprise. I won't try to resist. I can crawl off into the trees with my hands raw and my mouth full of snow and find a place to sleep for a small time. No need for you to worry. If you like it I can dream on a rich man's table with an apple in my mouth. I can be huge and win prizes for my body. None of it will bother me. Soon I'll have a pig's heart and know what I've been hungry for. I will smell it through the snow. My love, it will be better then. No pain at the start of the procedure. Then, my body with the chance to ache. Then with my clever ears I'll hear you coming every time you come to me. No words. Quick healing. Under the bright stitches, the slow march of a big two-fisted heart. At last you'll really lay your hands on me.

The list of the missing

1

Your daughter, she has the most beautiful blacksmith's hands I've ever seen. She will stand at the end of time with the gold hammer. Someone has to do it. Your daughter sucked meat from the bone and forgave everyone. It nearly killed her. I don't remember what she looks like running but I must have seen it. A photo in a bedside table, where she runs to meet the rare strangers of her future, tongue out, pummelling the low grass. Add that to the register. A girl in navy shorts, hounded through a gone summer. She has the hands of an accountant. Once she carried home an eggshell because it was so blue. It was so blue, there's no denying it. If I knew what was good for me I'd do it, and be a good girl running to be counted. Feed my neighbours by reaching through the letterbox, dry cereal heaped on my left palm. Most nights, she leads a horse along the low fence to the river and we never hear of it again, but in the city there are men with long ears, heavy shoes, branded skin. Torchlight, frantic in the dark. Don't shame a girl for trying.

2

Look, I have drawn up a list of my own. Daisy. Door keys. Lump of Hair. Book of addresses. Vast of snow. Tin of peaches. Widdershins. Mobile phone. Glass eye. Prize hen.

3

There are no ways of turning horses fully into men. They are not asking for forgiveness. They hear gunfire and they do not run to meet it. They go hungry. They go to the river. We do not know how to count the missing. Some men are horses. Some men are men. Some are made of paper. Some men are made of straw. Some men are full of pitch and tar. Add that to the official calculation. Give us all our portions of bread. Bread is easy. Bodies eat it. I have seen them do it. I have seen their talent for hunger. I have seen them sunk in the river.

4

Daisy, daisy, eggshell, cereal, hammer, snow, eyeball, hen, peaches, peaches, keys, keys, keys.

A promise

"Come, thick night"
  - Lady Macbeth. Macbeth, Act 1, Scene 5

Whatever you did, I love you. I'll help you bury the bodies.
I'll carry them from the car with the cloth over their faces.

Whatever you did I won't let them look at you. I'll pack their mouths
with earth. We both will smell like earth. Whatever you did I'll know

you by the smell of your body, like animals, separated, animals
who have to eat something at some point, animals who cannot help it.

I will listen to you talking in your sleep about the things you did.
I know you love me because you smell like earth like me, and sometimes

you round up people or pleading animals and kill them on our bed.
The bed we share is covered in the same claw marks. Look at me,

of course I'll do it, I'll hand you the knife, I'll read you the instructions.
You can catch any bird or animal and kill it on our bed.

I won't even wash my hands. It will be almost morning.
Everything will be in order, the washing on the balcony hung pale

and dry and patient as a row of ghosts, our children and our dogs hungry
for nothing. Dreaming even. I'll practise, I promise, I'll sink my hands into the dirt.

If they hang us both on the usual Tuesday from the trees
the earth-reek of your soul will yammer from the trees with mine.

Even in such crooked sunstruck days, when everyone knows
somebody whose mouth is full of earth, I still want something to believe in

without reason. Once I was terrified some love, slope-necked and heaving,
would crawl into my arms, and I would bury any body

worth remembering. But here I am, not afraid of anything,
carrying the shovel to the car.

When the rain comes it comes for you

In the North lands of the city
teenage girls were levitating
in their bedrooms.
Crockery was flung across the kitchen.
Cloud crawled toward them on all fours.

Everything they did before the rain came
was a way of summoning the rain.

Anna by the long mirror
playing with her scissors

or striking matches on the staircase
until the matches were all gone.

And quietly the girls
made useful items, silk and license plates
and crockery and knives and rope
and millions of silver forks.

They made small amounts of jewellery
and money disappear.

Long before the rain came
they were gone.
No one goes to look for them
or their small amounts of money

When the rain came
it was millions of silver forks,
falling.

I never sang like that before.
Wind bloating the ghost-sack of a torn sail.
Or buckets of stale and silver water
hauled up from a pit.
The tune that forks make
falling to the ground.

Oh honey, oh tablecloth,
oh iron bar, oh china plate,
oh moth wing, oh ribcage,
oh cloud, oh fork, oh knife,
oh girl of mine, oh child.

I can't wait to meet the cannibals

When I meet the cannibals they will choose me for their own, the actual
gentlemen who know I'm good for eating, who have written my name on
their list, who have chosen the part of me worth saving till last, who will do it
properly, who care about these things, they will remember my body completely,
talk to me, I only want to meet the cannibals, look at me, my shoulders and hips
are fully rotational, my earlobes separated from the skull, my legs carry me where
I tell them, I can drink a lot of water, I can wait in a dark room, I can stay very
still and very tender, I can name the normal amount of colours, I seem interested
in conversation, I cover my body to keep it warm, when I breathe I don't have to
concentrate, when I put my ear to the road or to a strong tree I hear no voices, I
avoid poisonous animals, I move my dirt into designated areas, I receive prizes
for guessing the weight of livestock, I play the lottery, I brush my hair, I recognise
the faces of people I have known, when I find a child in the street I leave it alone,
I lock the door, I eat milk products, I moisturise, I just can't wait to meet the
cannibals, they have chosen me, their hands so clean and elegant, the sleeves of
their second best shirts rolled up to their elbows, I will eat so much sugar if that
will please them, I will sleep in a milk bath, I will walk out over the ice, I will be
chosen when you choose me, if only you'd admit it, I know you are a cannibal,
I've waited for you all my life.

Paint chart

Sugarblacktooth. Bilgewater. Blood-under-skin blue.
Coffee grain on butcher sink. Panpipes. Red raw heel. Divot
of bush bird. Took fright. Jungle slicker. Dirty fork. Chalk
thirst pink. Reaching green. Cat stink. Pizza shop neon.
Claude glass. Untidy bean stem. Smoker's thumb.
Desert bluff. Burnt cake. Faded crown. Tonsil. New-fish-
in-the-deep-dark yellow. Spine. All that crashing rock.
His green shirt, don't you remember? His favourite green shirt.
That exact green.

The burning house

We met as children outside a burning house. Of course when you're a child you run to the burning house. You know how children are.

Bare-fingered shadows clutching at a yellow sky. The cleverness of oxygen, the clumsy bodies separated from their weight, brittle-black, cherish-boned, carried easy on the shoulders of the leaping wind.

The lights that seized the evening by the wrists, dragged it whole into the town square where everyone could see its nakedness.

For years you heard the voices of the people who lived once in the burning houses, blown wild through the yawning grass, chattering the stillness into rags.

Don't you remember? We were the clever children, and we ran towards the heat. We began to recognise nakedness. I wish I could tell you that I stepped across the embers to drag what you had loved into the street. Or that I too heard them calling.

Now you are sleeping. Your face pale and uncovered like a bowl of milk left on the windowsill to feed the insects and other wild things. You are beginning to look like your father.

From a great height: World, the shape of blue half-haloing a struck match. Wind, laughing from across the fields, cradles to its chest the embers of another year.

Brick by shining brick

God moves loud in the wreck. God hangs his best skin on the door handle before he enters the house. God writes his many names on the bathroom wall. God bites down bucktooth on a strip of leather as they separate his limbs from his body. God is pressed into a heavy book to preserve his scent and his colours. God howls out of a car window. God with broken glass in his feet. God with a handful of sunflower seeds. God settles on your chest in the night, you cannot move for the weight of him. God kisses the corners of your eyes. God walks naked into your ordinary dreams. God watches the ships low-hung and swaggering with fruit. God clamours with the jealous birds. God inspects the house for dust. God is very young again, on the beach, waiting for the oranges to wash up onto shore. God in the kitchen opening the top drawer, neck veins drilling down into the thin flowers of his shirt. God on the rooftop, whistling to himself. God remembers the smell of an orange. God flags down the last car out of here. God pries open the bonnet to drink the oil. God sells towels and hot water. God with syrup on his hands to attract the moths. God tilts up your chin to inspect your lovely neck. God examines pieces of clockwork, greening spools of copper wire, chars of plastic wrap. God shows you his missing fingers, the ones he lost in a bet. God a knot in a blue ribbon. God beckons the blackest harvest. God drags packs of bad children back into the sea. God bloodless and without lungs. God wakes to a sound in the dark. God walks in a city of water they will sing about forever. God watches the bubbles of his breath rise. God choosing a slice of cake and a new dress. God whose face we cannot remember. God's different names carved into the neck of every young tree. God in an empty house. God dancing in the dust-filled attic light, in a coat that someone could not carry with them. God a young tree green and weeping from the neck. God gathering the wreckage, brick by shining brick.

Winter: a biography

I'll admit I was raised in a red house by a woman with red hands on a bare hill,
where birds walked on the ground and it was always winter and death
did not exist. She never married. She knelt down on the ice. Her mouth
red as an axe swung through the stomach of a cat. She held a handful of seeds.
She buried them and expected nothing. Death did not exist. I couldn't read
but I nailed the book through its heart to a tree, and waited. Spring's surrender flag
rippled alabaster in the distance. Sharp sigh of horizon. Winter a thin murmur
of bone. You were there too, admit it. The brittle child of us riding the same song
witless and burning to the old bridge like a stolen car. Stars, waterlogged
and filthy in the river. Glossy, bloated nettles humming by the road.
Every Saturday a man in a red coat measured the shape of our skulls.
Every tree had someone to climb it with a dishcloth in their mouth
to wipe its shining branches leafless, black. I held the weight of snow
in my arms like a sleeping animal. We drove unwatched across the border.

Full knuckled summer struck me speechless. Forgive me if I've been a stranger
here. Once again it's winter, and you can sleep in my arms like snow.

Salt song

I

Birches quake and dribble, hooded in their shrivelled mist like monks come begging through the frost for bread. River a stiff knot. Midges dither at the shallows where the warmer rain gathers. Just beneath the earth, skinny iris heads revolt. The taste of air the sound of a spoon knocked against a tin cup. White sinewed sky contorts like a snake in a jar.

II

I love to lie like this. Feet in the weir waters. Sun slunk behind a cloud like a struck wasp crawling to a spoon of sugar. Everywhere the teeth, they cover the ground. Send down their hectic roots. Soon, new trees by the river and their pale new fruit.

III

Soldiers on their way home through the frozen wood sing so handsomely, make love, play dice with one another on the dry side of the road.

IV

I'll not run any longer. Yes. I want to lie right here. Come let me sing to you all the songs left in a green evening. Let me be a whole fool. Here is coltsfoot, madden, houseleek, feverfew. Sweat has left its salt on my body already. Salt is necessary and good.

Jubilation

Come and sleep beside me. A squall of weak-eyed birds bleat at the beery sea.
Lights, no longer wretched, groan in the harbour. Little boats, manless, drifting
back. Fuck me in a field of stunted corn. Moon a melted doll's head. Blueprints
for a birch tree etched on the wreckage of the sky. Early morning glowing
pigblood blue. Wet as wish coins heaped and gleaming at the bottom of a well.
I won't remember the sodden earth studded with shoes. I'll forget the blind sun
thrashing, naked as a gunner startled from his sleep. I will have my teeth in your
shoulder. I've already forgotten the whining of their old machines. I've buried
the clocks to silence them. I will mistake their songs for cattle I once heard calling
to each other through the frost. I fill my mouth with butter and salt. Milk stain.
Echo of rosehip. Fern. Pucker of fish. Peaches. Hard blush. Hibiscus. Good bread.
My hands are covered with milk. We are still young and kneeling. Take what you
want. Tell me your new name. A dry handful of hornets knock at the windows,
tapping out a draft of some rough sugar-searching music. A tune I almost
recognise.

Advice

Look at the people who lie in the street. Draw them like angels who fell there from a great height. Collect their feathers for later use. Name your firstborn after a bend in the river so it comes back to you. Agree to pose naked on the summer pavement. Master the techniques for packing light bulbs and preserving fish. Note their delicate skeletons. The gloss of their mouths. Their children scattered in the early dark. Measure the heft of the girl you were, who skinned rabbits on the high cliffs of a starving island. Identify good lace and fruit by the pound. Consider your neck. A string of jade, coral, pearl, jade. A hand you would recognise anywhere. Most boys cry alone. Most soldiers shoot to miss. Go to your husband. Go to the edge of the world, go see its same drunken yellow houses. Go, tell me what they make of you. Go to the guard you would recognise anywhere by the shape of his shoulders or the fine hairs on his upper lip. Go find the men people watch from their doorway. The men who undress before eating. Who remove their watches at night before they leave the house. Who remove their watches before they make love. Write down their names. Walk along the wire fence until you find a good place. Bury the book of names there until you need it. Go find the women with rough pustules raising their hands into books for blind men, the ones hung from the neck until dead. Go borrow their blunt instruments of beauty. Remember the girl packing a raw clutch of lightbulbs into a cardboard box. She handles the shadows like she would a soot-dark mouse running over her fingers. Hands weightless, unbitten. She'd recognise you anywhere.